THE ELEMENTS

The Lanthanides

Richard Beatty

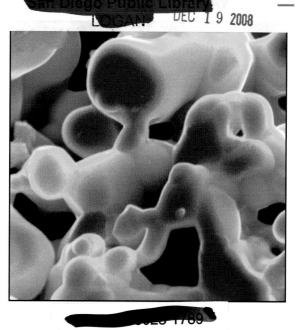

Marshall Cavendish
Benchmark
New York

Marshall Cavendish Benchmark
99 White Plains Road
Tarrytown, New York 10591

www.marshallcavendish.us

Library of Congress Cataloging-in-Publication Data

Beatty, Richard.
The Lanthanides / Richard Beatty.
        p.   cm – (The elements)
Includes index.
ISBN 978-0-7614-2687-5 (alk. paper)
1. Rare earth metals—Juvenile literature. I. Title.

QD172.R2B43 2007
546'.41—dc22

2006053053

1 6 5 4 3 2

Printed in Malaysia

Picture credits
Front cover: Shutterstock
Back cover: Shutterstock

Corbis: Carlos Cortes IV/Reuters 19, Peter Guttmann 11, Ted Streshinsky 5
2004 RGB Research Ltd.: www.element-collection.com 4, 9b
Shutterstock: Gerald Bernard 30, Andrey Chmelyor 23, Marc Dietrich 8, Jaimie Duplass 18, Glen Jones 27t,
Timothy Passmore 21, Andy Piatt 24, Ivan Stevanovic 22
Science Photo Library: 9t, 16, Michael W. Davidson 3, 14, Roberto De Gugliemo 12, Eye of Science 1, 26,
Astrid & Hanns-Frieder Michlet 15, Hank Morgan/University of Massachusetts at Amherst 25,
U.S. Dept. of Energy 27b, Zephyr 13.

Series created by The Brown Reference Group plc.
Designed by Sarah Williams
www.brownreference.com

Contents

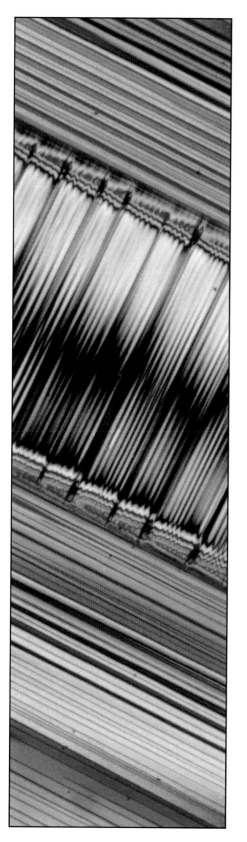

What are the lanthanides?

The lanthanides are a series of fifteen metal elements that are next to each other near the bottom of the periodic table. The name of the series comes from lanthanum, the element that marks the beginning of the series. All members of the series have similar chemical properties. In nature, they are found together in the same minerals, and they are difficult to separate into individual elements.

Until recently, there were few uses for the lanthanides, and chemists had little interest in them. Today, the opposite is true. Despite behaving in very similar ways during chemical reactions, the individual lanthanide elements have a huge range of other characteristics and uses. For example, some glow in a range of colors, and others can become magnetized.

Some of the latest modern technology uses the properties of purified lanthanide elements. For example, the red colors on a television screen are produced by the lanthanide element europium, while the most powerful magnets contain neodymium, another lanthanide.

A sample of lanthanum, the first element in the lanthanide series.

DID YOU KNOW?

RARE EARTHS

An alternative term for *lanthanide* is "rare earth." The word *earth* was once used by chemists for compounds now called oxides. A compound is formed when atoms of different elements bond together during a chemical reaction. An oxide is a compound that contains oxygen atoms. *Rare earth* was the term used for the oxides of lanthanide elements to distinguish them from better known earths, such as calcium oxide. Rare earths is not an ideal name, because some lanthanide elements, such as cerium and lanthanum are common in Earth's crust.

The metal yttrium (pronounced IT-ree-uhm) lies above the lanthanides in the periodic table, and it has similar properties to them. Yttrium is found in many of the same minerals as the lanthanides and is usually counted as a rare earth, too. Like many lanthanides, yttrium is important in lighting, televisions, and lasers.

Using a giant periodic table, a chemist points out the element holmium, one of the lanthanides. The lanthanides are positioned in a yellow-colored row beneath the rest of the periodic table.

Inside atoms

Like all elements, each lanthanide element consists of tiny atoms. Each atom has a small but heavy nucleus at its the center. The nucleus contains two types of particles: protons and neutrons. Protons have a positive charge. Neutrons are slightly larger than protons, but they have no charge—they are neutral. Electrons are a third type of particle found inside an atom. Electrons are much smaller than protons and neutrons. They are not inside the nucleus. Instead, they move around the nucleus in layers, or shells.

An electron has a negative charge that is equal and opposite to a proton's charge. Opposite charges attract, so electrons are held in place by a force that pulls them toward the nucleus. Each atom has an equal number of protons and electrons. The opposite charges cancel each other out, so an atom is neutral overall.

The atoms of the lanthanides

There are about 90 elements found in nature. When pure, each element is made up of a single type of atom. Each element

5

has atoms with a specific size and weight. Chemists describe an atom by the number of protons in its nucleus. That is called the atomic number. For example, the nucleus of an atom of lanthanum contains 57 protons. It has an atomic number of 57.

Each of the fifteen members of the lanthanide series has atoms with one more proton and one more electron than the member to the left of it. The series begins with lanthanum, with an atomic number of 57 and ends with lutetium, which has an atomic number of 71.

Adding electrons

The difference between most non-lanthanide elements is that an element with a higher atomic number has more electrons in the outer shell of its atoms. When the outer shell is full, a new shell is formed to hold more electrons.

An atom's outer electrons are the ones that take part in most chemical reactions. Elements have different chemical properties because they have different numbers of electron shells and outer electrons.

LANTHANUM ATOM

First shell	Fourth shell
Second shell	Fifth shell
Third shell	Sixth shell

The number of positively-charged protons in the nucleus of any atom is balanced by the number of negatively-charged electrons outside the nucleus. Lanthanum has 57 protons and 57 electrons. The electrons orbit the atom in 6 shells. There are 2 electrons in the first shell, 8 in the second, 18 in the third, 18 in the fourth, 9 in the fifth, and 2 in the sixth and outermost shell.

However, the lanthanide elements are different. They all have atoms with six electron shells, with one or two electrons in the outer shell. That is why the lanthanide elements behave in the same ways during chemical reactions.

If lanthanide elements with higher atomic numbers do not have more electrons in the outer shell, where do the extra electrons go? The answer is the fourth electron shell. This shell has room for 14 more electrons. Lanthanum has 18 electrons in the fourth shell. Lutetium has 32 electrons in that shell. The other 13 lanthanide elements have numbers in between.

Atomic differences

With such similar chemical properties, the main difference between the lanthanide elements is in the amount of space their atoms take up. The lanthanide elements with higher atomic numbers are actually smaller in volume than the lanthanides with lower atomic numbers.

LUTETIUM ATOM

Nucleus

First shell
Second shell
Third shell

Fourth shell
Fifth shell
Sixth shell

The number of positively-charged protons in the nucleus of any atom is the same as the number of negatively-charged electrons around it. A lutetium atom has 71 protons and 71 electrons. The electrons orbit the atom in 6 shells. There are 2 electrons in the first shell, 8 in the second, 18 in the third, 32 in the fourth, 9 in the fifth, and 2 in the sixth and outermost shell.

The lanthanide element dysprosium is used to make the reflective surface on compact discs.

Ionic compounds form when electrons move between the atoms. When an atom loses or gains one or more electrons, it becomes a charged ion. Atoms that lose electrons become positively-charged ions. Atoms that gain electrons become negatively charged ions.

Lanthanide atoms usually lose three electrons, forming an ion with a charge of +3. For example, lanthanum forms a La^{3+} ion. The electrons are transferred to the atoms of a nonmetal, such as oxygen (O_2). The oxygen atoms become oxide ions, which have a negative charge. The ions' opposite charges attract each other. The ions are held together by this attraction, and form a compound.

Atoms of most elements, including those of the lanthanides, come in several varieties called isotopes. An element's isotopes have different numbers of neutrons in their nuclei. The number of all particles in an atom's nucleus (the protons and neutrons) is the atomic mass number. For example, the most common isotope of cerium contains 58 protons and 82 neutrons, giving an atomic mass number of 140.

Lanthanide properties

Pure lanthanide elements are all silvery metals. They react with nonmetals such as oxygen, chlorine, or sulfur. Lanthanides form ionic compounds with nonmetals.

THE LANTHANIDE SERIES		
Atomic number	Name	Symbol
57	lanthanum	La
58	cerium	Ce
59	praseodymium	Pr
60	neodymium	Nd
61	promethium	Pm
62	samarium	Sm
63	europium	Eu
64	gadolinium	Gd
65	terbium	Tb
66	dysprosium	Dy
67	holmium	Ho
68	erbium	Er
69	thulium	Tm
70	ytterbium	Yb
71	lutetium	Lu

History of the lanthanides

At the end of the 1700s, the scientific study of chemistry was just beginning, and our understanding of the elements was beginning to take shape. People have known about some elements, such as gold, iron, and sulfur, since ancient times. Scientists eventually realized that many unknown elements were locked away in a variety of naturally-occurring compounds they called "earths."

The lanthanide story begins with the discovery of a new unknown mineral in a quarry in the village of Ytterby, near the

A sample of cerium. Cerium was the first member of the lanthanide series to be discovered. It is stored in a glass tube to stop it from reacting with the air.

KARL AUER VON WELSBACH

For most of the 1800s, lanthanide elements were of interest only to college chemists. That changed with the work of German chemist Karl Auer, Baron von Welsbach (1858–1929). Welsbach had discovered two lanthanides, praseodymium and neodymium. He also found the first practical use for the lanthanides.

Welsbach invented the gas mantle in the 1880s. That was a structure made from gauze (metal netting), which covered a gas flame. The gauze was made from thorium and the lanthanide cerium. The mantle made the gas flame glow more brightly. At the time, streetlamps were lit by gas flames, and Welsbach's mantle made them work more efficiently. Today, similar gas mantles are still used in camping lanterns.

Welsbach also invented an artificial flint used to make sparks for lighting flames. The flint contained mischmetal (a mixture of several lanthanide metals). When struck, this flint produced the spark that could light fires.

Swedish capital of Stockholm, in 1787. The mineral was investigated by Swedish chemist Johan Gadolin (1760–1852). In 1794, Gadolin announced that the mineral contained a new compound that he called yttria after the nearby village. The element yttrium was later obtained from this compound. Although yttrium is not actually a lanthanide, yttria was later shown to contain several genuine lanthanide elements, in smaller amounts.

A slow process

The first lanthanide to be discovered was cerium. That was found in a mineral called cerite in 1803. After that, new

---

DISCOVERING THE LANTHANIDES

The lanthanides were discovered over a long period of time. The dates below show the year in which each element was first discovered. In most cases, the elements were detected as part of a compound, such as an oxide. The pure metals were not extracted for many years afterward—nearly 100 years in some cases.

Year	Element	Origin or meaning of the name
1803	cerium	Ceres was the Roman god of corn, and was the first asteroid, discovered in 1801.
1839	lanthanum	An ancient Greek word meaning "to lurk," because lanthanum was "lurking" undetected in a cerium mineral
1843	erbium	The village of Ytterby
1843	terbium	The village of Ytterby
1878	holmium	Holmia is the Latin name for Stockholm, where it was discovered.
1878	ytterbium	The village of Ytterby
1879	samarium	The mineral samarskite (where the metal was first found) was named after Russian engineer Vasili Samarsky-Bykhovets (1803–1870)
1879	thulium	Thule is the Greek name for the far northern region of Europe that includes Scandinavia, where the metal was discovered.
1880	gadolinium	From the mineral gadolinite, which was named after chemist Johan Gadolin
1885	praseodymium	Meaning "lime-green didymium," since it was first discovered in the form of green compounds separated out from didymium (which was once thought to be an element itself)
1885	neodymium	"New didymium"
1886	dysprosium	Meaning "difficult to get," referring to how difficult it was to separate the element from holmium oxide
1901	europium	Named for the continent of Europe
1907	lutetium	Lutetia, the Latin name for Paris, where it was discovered
1938	promethium	Prometheus, the Greek god who brought fire to humankind

lanthanide elements were discovered throughout the nineteenth century. It took a long time because it was so difficult separate the elements out from each other.

Lanthanide elements are very similar, so early chemists did not find it easy to choose names for them all. Because four lanthanide elements were found in yttria, Ytterby ended up with the unique honor of having four elements named after it— yttrium, ytterbium, erbium, and terbium.

Swedish chemist Carl Gustav Mosander (1797–1858) discovered lanthanum in cerite in 1839 and then separated several other lanthanides from yttria. One of them he called didymium, but that was later found to be a mixture of several elements.

This statue of Prometheus is in New York City's Rockefeller Center. The lanthanide promethium is named for the god who stole fire from the gods and gave it to humans.

Using light

More lanthanide discoveries were helped by the new science of spectroscopy. That allowed unknown elements to be detected by the colors they produce when heated.

The final lanthanide to be discovered was promethium. All atoms of promethium are unstable, and they break apart and release radiation, which makes them radioactive. In 1938, promethium was the first element to be created artificially in a nuclear physics laboratory.

The lanthanides in nature

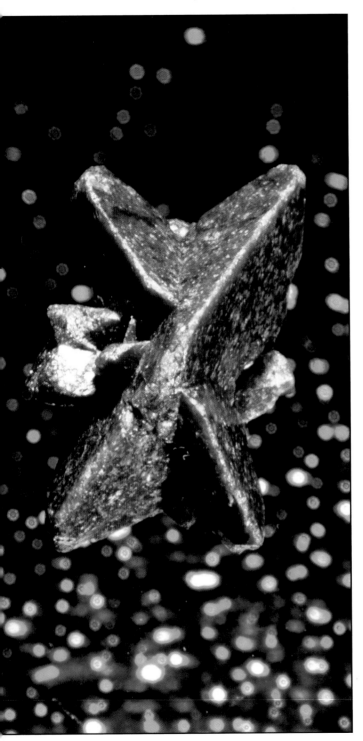

A crystal of monazite contains compounds of many lanthanide elements, including cerium, lanthanum, and neodymium.

Lanthanide elements are found throughout the universe, and astronomers can detect them by the light coming from distant stars. Not all the lanthanides are equally common. On Earth, cerium is the most common lanthanide, followed by neodymium and then lanthanum. The lanthanides are far too reactive to be found in their pure form as metals, so they exist naturally only as compounds.

Since Earth was formed, geological processes have grouped lanthanides together. They are found in the rocks that form the continents, rather than those under the ocean floor. Lanthanide compounds occur in rocks such as granite.

There are hundreds of different lanthanide-containing compound, but they usually occur in very small amounts. Only a few minerals contain large amounts of lanthanide compounds.

Bastnasite

Named for the Swedish town of Bastnäs where it was first found, bastnasite is a compound of lanthanide elements, carbon, oxygen, and fluorine. Scientists think bastanite forms in unusual geological circumstances, where magma (melted rock) cools underground in the presence of a lot of carbon dioxide gas. The most important known deposits of bastnasite occur at Mountain Pass, California, and in Inner Mongolia, in northern China.

Monazite and xenotime

Monazite is a lanthanide phosphate mineral (a compound containing phosphorus and oxygen). It occurs in small crystals in granite rock. When granite weathers (breaks up in the wind and rain), monazite

---

DID YOU KNOW?

LANTHANIDES AND LIVING THINGS

Lanthanide elements are found only in tiny amounts in plants and animals. That is because most of their natural compounds are insoluble (do not dissolve) in water, so plants cannot absorb them easily from the soil.

The lanthanides do not have any uses in the human body or in any other living thing. On the other hand, they do not seem to cause obvious harm either. Workers in lanthanide-processing plants, however, need to be careful not to breathe in dust containing lanthanide elements, which can cause lung problems.

---

crystals are carried away. The crystals are heavy so they soon settle to the ground. Many beaches in warm parts of the world have monazite in their sand. Monazite always contains some of the radioactive element thorium. That makes purifying monazite complicated because thorium is hard to separate from the mineral.

Xenotime is a mineral found in similar places to monazite, but it is more rare. Monazite contains lighter lanthanides, such as lanthanum and cerium. Xenotime contains more of the heavier elements in the series, such as dysprosium and lutetium.

Ionic ores

There are several other ores (useful minerals) containing ionic lanthanide compounds. Over millions of years, lanthanide ions have been carried in water from granite and trapped as individual ions in clay minerals. Most of these ores are mined in China.

An MRI scan shows a tumor in a prostate gland as an orange area. A gadolinium compound is injected into the gland to make it show up on the scan.

Mining and processing

This photo shows the surface of a crystal of lanthanum aluminate, an alloy of lanthanum and aluminum.

Getting lanthanide ores out of the ground and turning them into products is a complex process. Different minerals and ores are treated in a variety of ways, depending on what the final products will be. In addition, various methods are used in different countries.

Mining minerals

First, the ore must be taken out of the ground. In the case of monazite and xenotime, the most common method is to dig sand from lagoons using a ship called a dredger. The dredger contains equipment that shakes and sifts the sand so that heavier sand particles (including monazite and ores of other valuable metals) are separated out. The sand is separated in other ways on land until a large amount of monazite is gathered.

Bastnasite is dug up from open-pit mines, where miners dig away at the surface to make a huge hole. The bastnasite is not pure—it is mixed with other unwanted minerals. These are separated using flotation. All the minerals are crushed into a powder and mixed with soapy water. The soap forms foam, and the bastnasite clings to the bubbles. The unwanted minerals sink to the bottom.

Digestion

The next stage in most purification processes is called digestion. That involves reacting the concentrated ore with acids or alkalis. Acids, such as sulfuric acid, are highly reactive compounds that contain hydrogen ions (H^+). Alkalis, such as sodium hydroxide, are also reactive compounds, but they contain hydroxide ions (OH^-).

Digestion results in new lanthanide compounds, which have different properties from the ones in the ores. For example, when monazite is reacted with sodium hydroxide (NaOH), the lanthanide atoms form hydroxides. The hydroxides do not dissolve in water, so they form solid powders. However, the radioactive element thorium, which is also in monazite, still remains mixed with the lanthanides.

The mixture of hydroxides are then reacted with hydrochloric acid (HCl). The lanthanides form chlorides, which do dissolve. However, thorium hydroxide does not react with the acid, so it can now be separated out and removed.

Mixture of compounds

The mixture of lanthanide chlorides are dried into crystals. These compounds may be used to make mischmetal, an alloy that

Pitchblende, a mineral containing mainly uranium, is also a good source of cerium, the most common lanthanide element.

contains several lanthanide metals. (An alloy is a mixture of metals.) The mixture of lanthanide compounds are processed all together and turned into oxides or purified into metals.

In the case of ionic ores no digestion process is required. The lanthanide ions are washed out of the clay using salty water.

Separating elements

Pure lanthanides or their compounds are needed for many uses. The easiest lanthanide element to purify is the most common lanthanide element, cerium. Bastnasite, the main cerium-containing mineral, is often roasted before the digestion process. As it is heated, the cerium forms a new compound that is easier to separate.

The other lanthanides are so similar that ordinary chemical methods can not be used to separate them from each other.

The main difference between them is that their atoms vary in size. Over the years, separation techniques have been developed that make use of these differences.

The main method used today is called solvent-to-solvent extraction. A mixture of lanthanide compounds is dissolved in water. That is then pumped through another non-water liquid over and over again for a long time. The end result is that some lanthanides move from the water into the other liquid more quickly than others. So they can be gradually separated out. If done enough times, the process produces very pure samples of individual lanthanide compounds.

World production

In recent years there have been many changes in the production of lanthanide elements. For much of the twentieth century, the main source of lanthanides was the mineral monazite obtained from deposits of sands. In some cases, people were collecting other minerals, such as titanium ores, and monazite was collected at the same time.

Lanthanide compounds were produced as byproducts as the titanium ore was being processed. A byproduct is something that is made during the production of something else. However, the mixture of lanthanides also included the radioactive element thorium, which was not needed.

William F. Hillebrand

ATOMS AT WORK

Monazite is a mixture of phosphates, including thorium phosphate ($ThPO_4$) and phosphates of lanthanide elements. In the first stage of separating the elements, the phosphates are reacted with sodium hydroxide (NaOH).

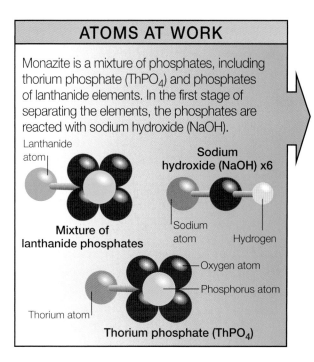

Lanthanide atom

Sodium hydroxide (NaOH) x6

Sodium atom

Hydrogen

Mixture of lanthanide phosphates

Oxygen atom

Phosphorus atom

Thorium atom

Thorium phosphate (ThPO$_4$)

The compounds are dissolved in water. They split into charged ions.

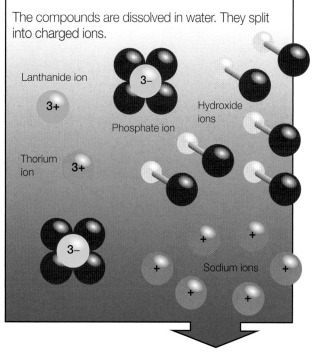

Lanthanide ion

3+

3−

Phosphate ion

Hydroxide ions

Thorium ion

3+

3−

+ +

+

+

Sodium ions

+

+ +

That caused problems with handling the radioactive waste products. As a result, the main sources of lanthanides have been changed to bastnasite and ionic ores.

Until the 1990s, the largest producer of bastnasite was a mine at Mountain Pass, California. Since then, a Chinese mine located at Bayan Obo, in Inner Mongolia, has become the world's biggest.

In China, bastnasite production started as a byproduct of mining for iron ore, and because Chinese miners are paid less than those in California and China has fewer laws to protect the environment, mining there is less expensive.

About 110,000 tons (100,000 tonnes) of rare-earth oxides (lanthanides plus yttrium) are mined each year. About 98 percent of this comes from China.

The hydroxide ions form compounds with the lanthanide and thorium ions. These compounds do not dissolve, and they form crystals that sink to the bottom. The sodium and phosphate ions stay dissolved in the water.

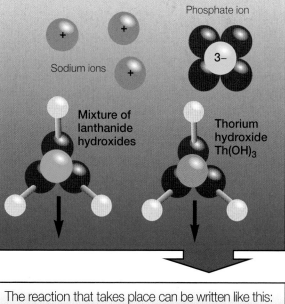

Phosphate ion

+   +

Sodium ions

+

3−

Mixture of lanthanide hydroxides

Thorium hydroxide Th(OH)$_3$

The reaction that takes place can be written like this:

LanthanidePO$_4$ + ThPO$_4$ + 6NaOH → Lanthanide(OH)$_3$ + Th(OH)$_3$ + 2Na$_3$PO$_4$

Metals and alloys

If you tried to build an automobile using pure lanthanide metals, you would not get very far. Most of the pure lanthanide elements are so soft that they can be cut with a steel knife, and they are far too reactive to stay pure for long. Combined into alloys with other metals, however, lanthanides have become very important to modern technology.

Metallic properties

Pure lanthanide metals are shiny and silvery. However, they tarnish (become dull) quickly in air as they form a gray coating or powder of metal oxide.

Lutetium, the last in the series, is the hardest and least reactive. It also has the highest melting point of all lanthanides (3,025 °F or 1,663 °C). It is also the most expensive metal in the world to produce, so its uses are limited. Europium is the most reactive lanthanide, and has the lowest melting point (1,511 °F or 822 °C). If heated in air, europium will burst into flames. In the laboratory, pure lanthanide metals have to be kept under oil or in an unreactive gas to stop them from reacting.

Purification

Extracting pure metals from lanthanide compounds is a difficult task. Lanthanides bond so strongly to oxygen and other nonmetals that they cannot be smelted like iron ore. During smelting, carbon reacts with metal oxides. The carbon strips the oxygen away from the metal atoms to make carbon dioxide and pure metal.

The magnets used in small electronic devices, such as portable computers and headphones, contain mixtures of lanthanide metals.

In the case of the lanthanide, two other purification methods are used instead: metallothermic reduction and electrolysis.

Metallothermic reduction can be used to obtain any of the lanthanide elements. First, a compound containing a single lanthanide is made and reacted with fluorine to make a compound called a fluoride. Calcium, a reactive metal, is added to the mixture. The calcium reacts with the fluoride to make calcium fluoride. Atoms of lanthanide metal are left behind.

Electrolysis is a method that uses electricity to pull compounds apart into separate atoms. The electricity is passed through a melted lanthanide chloride or fluoride. This method is used for the lighter lanthanides, such as lanthanum and neodymium. These metals melt at low temperatures, making electrolysis easier.

A worker inspects rolls of steel at a steelworks in China. Chinese steel is purified using lanthanides.

Mischmetal

Because individual lanthanides are so difficult to purify, the first practical use of the metals was in so-called mischmetal (from the German word for "mixed metal"). Mischmetal is an alloy containing lanthanides in the same proportions as in the ore it is extracted from. That is typically about 50 percent cerium, 25 percent lanthanum, and 25 percent of all the rest.

Mischmetal alloyed with iron is used to make the flints that spark in cigarette lighters. Mischmetal is also important in steelmaking. It is added to steel, in which the lanthanides elements remove unwanted impurities. This use is still important in China, where lanthanide

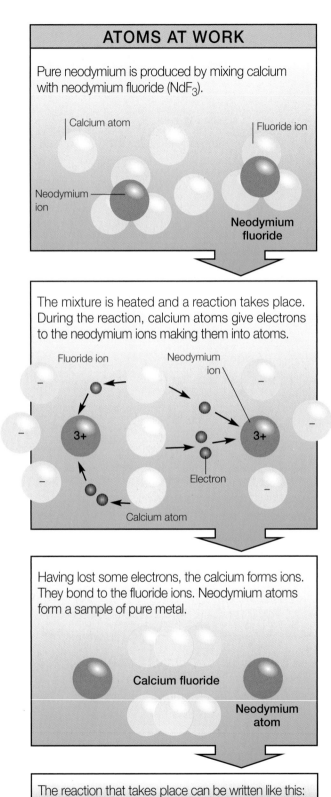

ATOMS AT WORK

Pure neodymium is produced by mixing calcium with neodymium fluoride (NdF_3).

Calcium atom

Fluoride ion

Neodymium ion

Neodymium fluoride

The mixture is heated and a reaction takes place. During the reaction, calcium atoms give electrons to the neodymium ions making them into atoms.

Fluoride ion

Neodymium ion

3+

3+

Electron

Calcium atom

Having lost some electrons, the calcium forms ions. They bond to the fluoride ions. Neodymium atoms form a sample of pure metal.

Calcium fluoride

Neodymium atom

The reaction that takes place can be written like this:

$$3Ca + 2NdF_3 \rightarrow 3CaF_2 + 2Nd$$

ores are more common than in most other countries. Steelworks in other parts of the world remove impurities in other ways.

Mischmetal is used for many other purposes, such as in batteries. However, in most mischmetals, the heavier lanthanides (samarium to lutetium) have been separated out.

Powerful magnets

Some lanthanide metals are used to make the world's most powerful permanent magnets. Permanent magnets are those that are magnetic all the time. Electromagnets work only when an electric current is passed through them.

Pure lanthanide magnets work only at very low temperatures. However, when combined into alloys, the lanthanides form more practical magnets that have helped to revolutionize the electronics industry. It is lanthanide-containing magnets that make it possible to have tiny headphones small enough to fit into the ear, as well as small, lightweight hard disk drives for use in laptops or MP3 players. The alloys are used in larger magnets, too.

The first lanthanide magnets were developed in the early 1970s. They were an alloy of samarium and cobalt. In the mid–1980s, an even more powerful type of magnet was invented that contained neodymium, iron, and boron. These "neo" magnets are now found everywhere in

ATOMS AT WORK

Powerful magnets are made from an alloy of samarium and cobalt. This alloy is produced by mixing samarium oxide (Sm_2O_3) with pure cobalt and pure calcium.

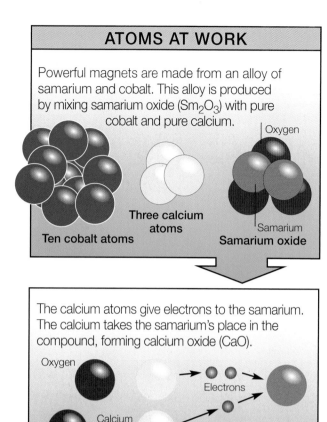

Ten cobalt atoms

Three calcium atoms

Oxygen

Samarium

Samarium oxide

The calcium atoms give electrons to the samarium. The calcium takes the samarium's place in the compound, forming calcium oxide (CaO).

Oxygen

Calcium

Electrons

Samarium

Each samarium atom mixes with five cobalt atoms to form an alloy ($SmCo_5$).

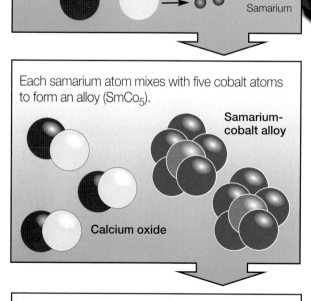

Samarium-cobalt alloy

Calcium oxide

The reaction that takes place can be written like this:

$$3Ca + 10Co + Sm_2O_3 \rightarrow 2SmCo_5 + 3CaO$$

today's machines, and have had the effect of greatly increasing the world's demand for neodymium.

Other uses of alloys

Alloys of lanthanides are used in a number of other areas. For example, they are used to strengthen magnesium alloys. Certain lanthanides are also an ingredient in a new type of rechargeable batteries. Some lanthanides can also be used in memory cards and other electronic storage devices.

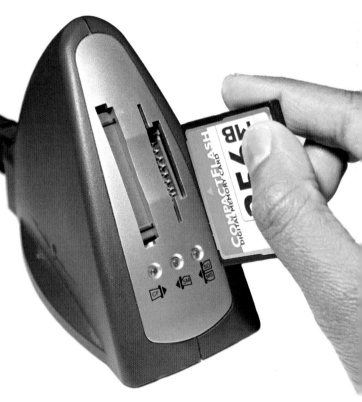

A memory card containing images taken with a digital camera makes use of the properties of the lanthanide element terbium.

Light, color, and lasers

The light used to make pictures on flat plasma screens is produced using lanthanide compounds.

The lanthanide elements are used in many of the new ways of artificially creating light and color. Today there are many other sources of light, such as flat plasma screens, dashboards lit up by light-emitting diodes (LEDs), and lasers.

Light and atoms

Light is part of what scientists call electromagnetic radiation. That also includes other radiation, such as radio waves, heat, and X rays.

Light is a series of waves. Waves are measured in three ways: speed, wavelength, and frequency. Light has a fixed speed, known as the speed of light. Its waves always travels at this speed. The wavelength is the distance between the top

of one wave and the one behind it. For example, an ocean wave might have a wavelength of several yards. A wave's frequency is the number of times a wave travels its wavelength each second.

All light travels at the same speed, so a light wave with a long wavelength can only cover a few of them in a second. Thus it has a low frequency. Light with a shorter wavelength covers more of them per second and has a higher frequency.

The eye can detect light of different frequencies, which we then see as colors. For example, blue light has a higher frequency than red light. Light made up of all frequencies, or colors, appears white.

Light waves are produced by atoms. When energy is added to an atom, it can cause one of the atom's electrons to jump from an inner electron shell to one farther out. The electron then falls back again to its normal position, and a wave of light is released. Each atom produces particular frequencies, or colors, of light. That is why elements and compounds burn with characteristic colors when they are heated. Light from light bulbs, lasers, or televisions are produced in the same way.

Efficient lighting

The light from a normal light bulb is produced by a metal filament that is heated by an electric current so that it glows white hot. That is a wasteful way of making light because the light bulb also produces a lot of heat, which is invisible.

Fluorescent bulbs are more efficient because they create light without producing wasted heat. Fluorescent bulbs are tubes of gas without filaments. When an electric current runs through the gas, it produces invisible ultraviolet (UV) light. UV light has a higher frequency than visible light.

The UV rays hit a coating inside the bulb's tube. This coating gives off visible light. Substances that behave like this are called phosphors. Lanthanide elements such as europium and terbium make excellent phosphors. Their atomic structure allows them to emit bright colors.

Modern fluorescent bulbs usually have a coating of several different phosphors. Among them, the light they create combines into a whitish light.

Light-emitting diodes (LEDs) operate quite differently. They are based on a solid substance that glows when electricity is passed through it. The most common LED

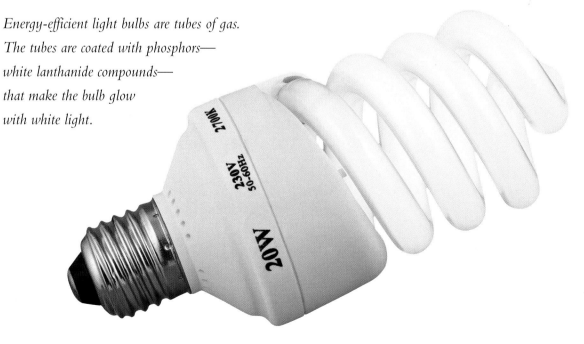

Energy-efficient light bulbs are tubes of gas. The tubes are coated with phosphors— white lanthanide compounds— that make the bulb glow with white light.

ATOMS AT WORK

Fluorescent light bulbs are filled with atoms of argon gas. When the bulb is switched on, an electric current knocks electrons off the gas atoms, producing a stream of ions and electrons.

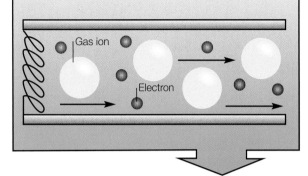

The gas ions and electrons smash into mercury atoms in the bulb. The mercury atoms release ultraviolet (UV) light. The UV light is invisible.

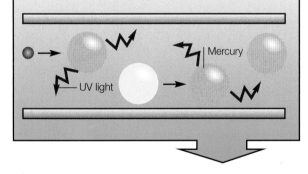

Rays of UV light hit a layer of phosphor that coats the inside of the light bulb. The phosphor contains atoms of lanthanide elements. When the invisible UV light shines onto the phosphor, it is converted into visible light. This light shines out of the bulb making it glow brightly.

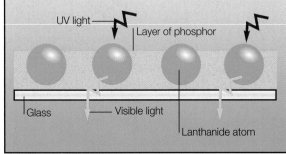

DID YOU KNOW?

REFLECTING COLORS

The lanthanides are just as good at absorbing particular light frequencies as they are at giving them out. Paints, dyes, and other colored materials with lanthanides in them have a certain color because they absorb only some frequencies of the white light that falls on them. The rest of the light is reflected back. This reflected light is missing certain frequencies. As a result, it is no longer white but has a particular color that you see. Adding a lanthanide, such as erbium, praseodymium, or neodymium, to pottery or glassware creates pink, green, and purple colors. Paints and plastics are colored red and orange using a range of pigments (colored materials) based on cerium sulfide.

Some marbles are colored by lanthanides that are mixed into the glass.

glows blue, but this can be turned into white or many other colors by coating that with a phosphor containing cerium

Glowing screens

Older televisions and computer monitors produce images using a beam of electrons. The beam shines a pattern onto the back of the screen, which is covered in phosphor. The phosphors glow in that pattern and form an image. Color television screens have three kinds of phosphor that glow in red, green, and blue. The red phosphor uses europium, combined into an yttrium-containing compound. Europium is also used in modern flat plasma screens.

Lasers

Invented in the late 1950s, lasers produce light in yet another way. They add energy to a group of identical atoms. As a result, the atoms are all in the same excited state that makes their electrons move up into outer electron shells. An electron dropping back to a lower shell gives out light of a particular color. That light stimulates nearby atoms to give out the same light in a chain reaction. This results in an intense beam of light that is made up of waves with exactly the same frequency, or color.

There are many different lasers. Some lasers make light with gases, others use solids. The sharp colors produced by lanthanides make them suitable for solid lasers. Lasers based on neodymium are common. A neodymium laser is usually an invisible beam of heat, which can be used to mark or cut metal. However, neodymium lasers can also produce green light.

A green neodymium laser beam reflects between several mirrors.

Other uses

The lanthanides also play many roles in modern industry and technology. They are commonly used as catalysts. Catalysts are substances that help certain chemical reactions take place. Other applications range from the nuclear industry to creating imitation jewelry.

Getting a reaction

A catalyst takes part in chemical reactions but it is not changed or used up in the process. A mixture of lanthanide elements is used as the catalyst for "cracking" crude oil. Cracking is the process that breaks the large compounds in the oil into simpler substances that are more useful. Gasoline and other fuels are produced in this way.

Cerium oxide is one of the catalysts in the catalytic converters of automobiles and road vehicles. Along with other other oxides and precious metals such as platinum, cerium oxide removes pollution and dangerous gases from the exhaust.

In this image, a superconductor containing lanthanum is magnified 6,000 times. Unlike other conductors, this material does not warm up when electrified.

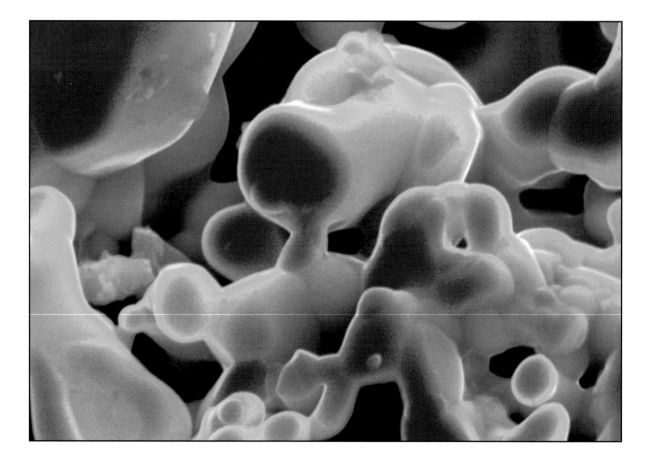

Looking at glass

Other uses of lanthanides include various roles in glassmaking. Cerium oxide is a very hard substance, and in powdered form it is used to polish glass. The compound can also be added to the glass to clear away iron-containing impurities that discolor the glass. Adding other lanthanide compounds to glass can change the way the glass bends light. That type of glass is used to filter out harmful rays, such as ultraviolet light.

Specialized uses

The lanthanides also have various specialized uses in medical imaging equipment, as well as in the nuclear industry. One role lanthanides play

A welder wears a protective hood, which contains a dark visor to protect his eyes from the brightness of the sparks. The dark visor contains neodymium.

in nuclear reactors is absorbing stray radiation, especially neutrons that are released by radioactive materials. Gadolinium is particularly effective at absorbing neutrons.

Some semiconductors—materials used in microchips and other electronics—have tiny amounts of lanthanide elements added to them to make them work better. Lanthanide oxides also strengthen crystals of zirconia (zirconium oxide). Zirconia is a very hard substance used in cutting tools and in fake diamonds.

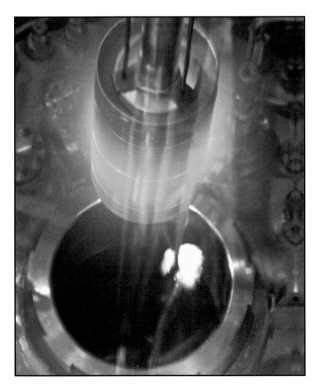

Nuclear fuel is added to a nuclear reactor. The fuel contains small amounts of gadolinium, which stops the fuel from burning away too quickly.

Periodic table

Everything in the universe is made from combinations of substances called elements. Elements are made of tiny atoms, which are too small to see. Atoms are the building blocks of matter.

The character of an atom depends on how many even tinier particles called protons there are in its center, or nucleus. An element's atomic number is the same as the number of its protons.

Scientists have found around 116 different elements. About 90 elements occur naturally on Earth. The rest have been made in experiments.

All these elements are set out on a chart called the periodic table. This lists all the elements in order according to their atomic number.

The elements at the left of the table are metals. Those at the right are nonmetals. Between the metals and the nonmetals are the metalloids, which sometimes act like metals and sometimes like nonmetals.

- On the left of the table are the alkali metals. These have just one outer electron.

- Metals get more reactive as you go down a group. The most reactive nonmetals are at the top of the table.

- On the right of the periodic table are the noble gases. These elements have full outer shells.

- The number of electrons orbiting the nucleus increases down each group.

- Elements in the same group have the same number of electrons in their outer shells.

- The transition metals are in the middle of the table, between Groups II and III.

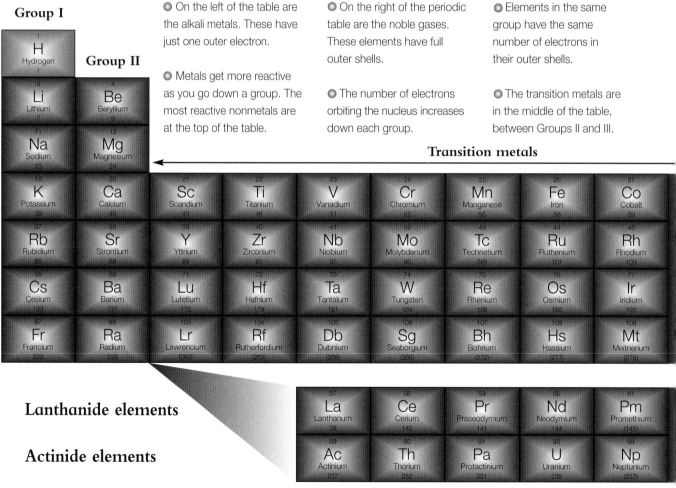

Transition metals

Group I

Group II

Lanthanide elements

Actinide elements

The horizontal rows are called periods. As you go across a period, the atomic number increases by one from each element to the next. The vertical columns are called groups. Elements get heavier as you go down a group. All the elements in a group have the same number of electrons in their outer shells. This means they react in similar ways.

The transition metals fall between Groups II and III. Their electron shells fill up in an unusual way. The lanthanide elements and the actinide elements are set apart from the main table to make it easier to read. All the lanthanide elements and the actinide elements are quite rare.

The lanthanide elements

The lanthanides are a series of elements from lanthanum to lutetium. They are generally listed below the main periodic table. The atoms of the lanthanide elements have six electron shells. They have 1 or 2 electrons in the sixth shell and 8 or 9 in the fifth. However, there are between 18 and 32 electrons in the fourth shell.

Metals
Metalloids (semimetals)
Nonmetals

						Group VIII
						2 He Helium 4

Atomic (proton) number
57
La
Symbol
Lanthanum
Name
39
Atomic mass

Group III	Group IV	Group V	Group VI	Group VII	
5 B Boron 11	6 C Carbon 12	7 N Nitrogen 14	8 O Oxygen 16	9 F Fluorine 19	10 Ne Neon 20
13 Al Aluminum 27	14 Si Silicon 28	15 P Phosphorus 31	16 S Sulfur 32	17 Cl Chlorine 35	18 Ar Argon 40

28 Ni Nickel 59	29 Cu Copper 64	30 Zn Zinc 65	31 Ga Gallium 70	32 Ge Germanium 73	33 As Arsenic 75	34 Se Selenium 79	35 Br Bromine 80	36 Kr Krypton 84
46 Pd Palladium 106	47 Ag Silver 108	48 Cd Cadmium 112	49 In Indium 115	50 Sn Tin 119	51 Sb Antimony 122	52 Te Tellurium 128	53 I Iodine 127	54 Xe Xenon 131
78 Pt Platinum 195	79 Au Gold 197	80 Hg Mercury 201	81 Tl Thallium 204	82 Pb Lead 207	83 Bi Bismuth 209	84 Po Polonium (209)	85 At Astatine (210)	86 Rn Radon (222)
110 Ds Darmstadtium (281)	111 Rg Roentgenium (280)	112 Uub Ununbium (285)	113 Uut Ununtrium (284)	114 Uuq Ununquadium (289)	115 Uup Ununpentium (288)	116 Uuh Ununhexium (292)		

62 Sm Samarium 150	63 Eu Europium 152	64 Gd Gadolinium 157	65 Tb Terbium 159	66 Dy Dysprosium 163	67 Ho Holmium 165	68 Er Erbium 167	69 Tm Thulium 169	70 Yb Ytterbium 173
94 Pu Plutonium (244)	95 Am Americium (243)	96 Cm Curium (247)	97 Bk Berkelium (247)	98 Cf Californium (251)	99 Es Einsteinium (252)	100 Fm Fermium (257)	101 Md Mendelevium (258)	102 No Nobelium (259)

Chemical reactions

Chemical reactions are going on around us all the time. Some reactions involve just two substances, while others involve many more. In a chemical reaction, the number and type of atoms stay the same. They join up in new combinations to form molecules.

Writing an equation

Chemical reactions can be described by writing down the combinations of atoms and molecules before and after the

An oil refinery uses catalysts containing lanthanide compounds in order to help certain reactions take place.

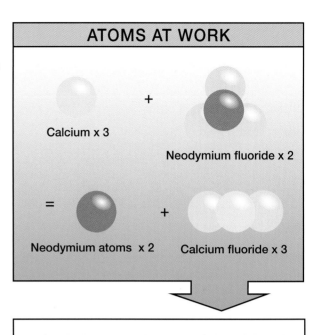

ATOMS AT WORK

Calcium x 3

+

Neodymium fluoride x 2

=

Neodymium atoms x 2

+

Calcium fluoride x 3

The reaction that takes place when calcium reacts with neodymium fluoride is written like this:

3Ca + 2NdFl$_3$ → 3CaFl$_2$ + 2Nd

This tells us that three atoms of calcium reacts with two molecules of neodymium fluoride to give three molecules of calcium fluoride and two atoms of neodymium.

reaction. Since the atoms stay the same, the number of atoms before and after the reaction will be the same. Chemists write the reaction as an equation. This shows what happens in the chemical reaction.

Making it balance

When the numbers of each atom on both sides of the equation are equal, the equation is balanced. If the numbers are not equal, something is wrong. The chemist adjusts the number of atoms involved until the equation balances.

Glossary

acid: A chemical that releases hydrogen ions when dissolved.

alkali: A compound that neutralizes an acid, producing water and a compound known as a salt.

atom: The smallest part of an element having all the properties of that element. Each atom is less than a millionth of an inch in diameter.

atomic mass number: The number of protons and neutrons in an atom.

atomic number: The number of protons in an atom.

bond: The sharing or exchange of electrons between atoms that holds them together to form molecules.

compound: A substance made of atoms of more than one element. The atoms are held together by chemical bonds.

crystal: A solid consisting of a repeating pattern of atoms, ions, or molecules.

dissolve: When a solid substance mixes with a liquid, or solvent, very evenly so that the solid disappears.

electrolysis: The use of electricity to break the bonds between atoms in a compound to make pure elements.

electron: A tiny particle with a negative charge. Electrons are found inside atoms, where they move around the nucleus in layers called electron shells.

element: A substance that is made from only one type of atom.

ion: An atom or molecule that has lost or gained electrons. This gives it a negative or positive electrical charge.

isotopes: Atoms of an element with the same number of protons and electrons but different numbers of neutrons.

metal: A hard and shiny element that is good at conducting heat and electricity. All the lanthanides are metals.

neutron: A tiny particle with no electrical charge. Neutrons are found in the nucleus of every element except hydrogen.

nonmetal: An element on the right-hand side of the periodic table.

nucleus: The dense structure at the center of an atom. Protons and neutrons are found inside the nucleus of an atom.

ore: A mineral or rock that contains enough of a particular substance to make it useful for mining.

periodic table: A chart of all the chemical elements laid out in order of their atomic number.

proton: A tiny particle with a positive charge. Protons are found inside the nucleus of an atom.

radioactivity: A property of certain unstable atoms that causes them to release radiation.

reaction: A process in which two or more elements or compounds combine to produce new substances.

Index